CW00502175

# AUTOLINGO DIDACTICA

JORDAN/MARTIN HELL

*In my platforms I hit the floor / fell face down / it didn't help
my brain out / then the curtain came before I found / the
magic how / to keep you happy / I never was the fantasy /
of what you wanted me to be …*

   *Playboy Mommy*, Tori Amos

I probably should never have seen *Harold & Maude* but of course I watched it for the first time when I was 10 years old. I think it gave me all the wrong ideas about love & relationships. If you're not familiar, it's a zany rom-com about a 20-year-old vaguely goth boy obsessed with faking his own suicide to agitate his eccentric conservative socialite mother. **\*SPOILER ALERT\*** In the end he falls in love with a free-spirited & kooky badass elderly aristocratic woman (played by the incomparable Ruth Gordon) who he's determined to marry until she happily kills herself for basically no reason on her 80th birthday in order to die on her own devil-may-care terms. Despite the premise, the film is uproariously funny & profound as hell. Either way, in addition to a MILF / GILF complex it also gave me hope.

At 12 I began to follow my 7th grade teacher home from school. Her name was Mindy. She had a son who had a severe learning disability. She'd go for runs most days at lunch time home to go check on him & come back to school sweaty in pink or orange Adidas gym shorts, then change into dress pants for the afternoon's lessons. Running after her when she left, about a block or so behind because I was slow & I knew where she was going, I'd huff along & feel the breeze like a caress as it wove through my hair & my shirt clung, jiggling on my husky tummy & tiny new breasts. When I'd get there, to her house, I'd watch through the window while she played with the boy or fed him lunch. I never once saw her kiss her wife. Years later, in high school, I saw her at Pride & realized she'd had one the whole time & that she was as gay as I always hoped she was. I wasn't the only one. Lots of girls & boys talked about her. She was well-liked among the students. But in terms of the fanatical zeal I displayed, only one matched me. Her name was Ashley & she looked like Gollum from *Lord of the Rings*. She was also crass. She harassed Mindy with affection. Back then it embarrassed me. On days when I wasn't following Mindy, the two of us would stand outside her classroom & wait for her return. When she'd let us in early to hang around & chat shit, Ashley was always the first one hustling through the door, haggling for social credit by bragging about her nonsensical online anime life. On the last day of school, I sobbed uncontrollably in the arms of a frenemy with the weight of the world on my shoulders all because I was moving up a grade & so would have to leave her behind.

But the next year I met Ms. Kane whom I never called by her first name, even once I figured out what it was, because she was formidable & violently more addictive. She was also from Honolulu, Hawaii, which seemed impossible at the time because to us hillbilly children Honolulu, Hawaii, was a fantasy destination on an imaginary map, not a hometown. In the new building our school moved to that year, 8th grade was in a row of classrooms on a balcony. For me, that meant that if I stood in a certain spot in the hallway I could eyeball Mindy with one eye & Ms. Kane with the other. This of course led to emotional disaster almost immediately.

Nevertheless, I kept my post until I graduated. What can I say? Though the toll of psychic agony nearly drove me to suicide, it *also* gave me hope.

I imagined all the teachers had an inner circle with an inner life, secular & separated from us kids like the surgical residents from *Grey's Anatomy* who hung out at the local fictional bar called Joe's or in the basement hallway to where the cadavers were kept, sometimes eating chips, drinking beer, & talking shop; healing & helping each other through whatever traumas being a middle school teacher happened to afford a person. In fact, I found out from some other children that they all were rumored to nightcap after work at a bar nearby. I drowned in envy & intrigue thinking of what they might be discussing between every cheers. It never crossed my mind that it might be me. I'm serious. I knew my place like any respectable fan. My job was to hoover gossip & spring delusions forth from air, not to actually *know* them or be known by them. That wasn't even desirable. Longing for the inner world of the women who taught me was in part about a longing for a life of my own, much more than I would readily admit. Like any stalker I was jealous as a thief. I wanted the freedom they had & the relative peace but in a new mind & body, one that could actually enjoy it.

Being an adult woman seemed to mean you always had a special case of perfumed beauty cream in your back pocket & a French sheen on your perfectly coiffed hair that directly correlated to your uncanny ability to turn any household phrase into a 5-star bridal bouquet in 7 seconds or less. As far as I could tell, womanhood was all about blending lipsticks with liners while holding your ankles together & looking clean in Banana Republic. Real women had jobs which didn't deflect from their ability to smile & wink in such a way as to cause fatal cardiac arrests or engender marriage proposals from eligible clergymen. They drove either Volkswagen Beetles or Jeeps in either powder pink, baby blue, or some dark sultry earth color that perpetually matched their fingernails & wore their sexy designer librarian glasses with a certain joie de vivre as they crossed from the overhead projector to the pencil sharpener to admonish you for daydreaming. They were better, faster, smarter, stronger, older, colder, cooler, better educated, & more worthy than I was or could ever be in my bedazzled rayon bralette which I'd accidentally broken like the Incredible Hulk from mindlessly over-stretching it out with my stupid boobs. I desperately hated my tits, such as they were. They were meant to be my greatest asset but turned out to be a major liability even then. It was cruel. They were like tumors in residence, stuck onto me like evil barnacles or freeloading parasites, marking an obscenely warped nude-y line between me & everything. What's more, the absurdity of their presence made me an even worse woman than I already was by solidifying as document some claim I obviously had made long before even being born about wanting so badly to be a hot girl that I didn't care if I ended up failing completely as a TOTAL FUCKING *FREAK*! But none of my teachers ever talked about feeling like *that*. They'd have sooner committed hari-kari, I guess.

Being a certified creep felt like a part of the gay lexicon of embodiments that I could slip into if I ever felt too scared to be brave or annoying. The other gay kids were so much chiller & less shame-based than me. They all had supportive family members who helped them duct tape their mouths & write "NO H8!" in Sharpie on the almost weekly episodic National LGBT days of silence that inevitably would roll around & plague our classroom with their wordlessly marginal weak-ass brand of countercultural pestilence. I was of the mind to either be a fully functional digit of society's mighty fist, crushing the proverbial little guy, or be a total degenerate, which is to say, nothing at all. My dream was to either be a lawyer or a junkie prostitute & somehow I did manage to find ways to become petite versions of both (the latter much more properly than the former) but nothing about those lives really turned out how I thought they would be. The sex work I did was really wholesome & radical & well supported. As for the rock bottom I suffered from as a result of the alcoholism/drug addiction I'm now recovering from, it wasn't really all that terrible either. It took me getting sober to basically realize that it was my *actual* life that sucked, not the one of my dreams. The one I literally *lived* instead of visited, or *didn't* live but occupied nonetheless. The one where I was vulnerable & sad & broken & wrong, or thought I was because I had been victimized, suppressed, broken, wronged, & made to think I was less than nothing my whole life & I believed it. I believed it because I didn't know any better. I didn't know any better because I didn't know *anyone*. I only knew things *about* people.

Before the internet, there was the telephone. In Ohio, even in the midst of the internet, the telephone still reigned perhaps a decade or so longer than some other places because it was more accessible. But more powerful than both those things was the mall & to a much lesser extent in my specific world, the show. As a loner with less than no interest in my fellow youths, going to the mall (though necessary) was a bit of a non-event. I didn't know or care who was sleeping with whom, most TV references went over my head as I mainly read books, listened to vinyl records, wrote on my typewriter, & watched films either on an old school reel-to-reel projector or on VHS which was very uncool. In the early aughts, Blu-ray discs & 3D movies were the final word in media. I couldn't watch 3D movies because the glasses gave me vertigo, so I usually just rode my bike around or went to punk shows. By punk I really mean a vast & eclectic range of music which encompassed everything from the very avant-garde & virtuosic experimentalisms of classically trained theremin protégés to this one guy in town who would line up a wall of Marshall amps at full capacity with about a hundred distortion pedals daisy-chained to a mic he'd then fart into with a seriousness & narcissistic conceit that would put

12

any Metallica-minded thrasher band of impotent jerk-offs to shame. Most often though the bands were really amazing & just crazy fun. Luckily it was a world I'd strangely been inducted into as a local legend of sorts, being that I was so young & had played shows in bars with more than decent crowds & line-ups since I was even younger.

*There is no human hope without the promise of ecstasy.*

Amber Hollibaugh

The thing about that kind of punk is that it is expansive & it expands you, sometimes in glorious ways, like the amplification of a deep inner power sends a flurry of kinetic imaginative truth through the body, a billowing silo filled with concerted emotion widening your insides & pouring them out of your mouth, the best kind of vomit – vomit of fear, of loss, of hurt, of longing, of living, of dying in order to breathe anew in ways that are purer, stronger, wilder than before. Then again, sometimes punk like that can be akin to being wrenched upon a rack of the Spanish Inquisition or burned at the stake, but less like a witch & more like a pig on a spit. It depends on your shame level & the spiral that creates & how you learn or resist change & effort. The fact remains that whatever way I took the lesson, punk was disciplining me in the epic trade of survival by any means necessary. It was teaching me that bars, basements, the street, & anywhere I could jam myself into was a place I could use to essentially go berserk so long as I had some element of art in it & I gave everything. As a hardcore absurdist (& schizophrenic antisocialite) I was easy with the public performance of rage (via lament) & wreckage because girls (or fidgety people who looked like girls) were *supposed* to be sad, were supposed to marry melancholia to their makeup, cake it on even. If they were sad enough, they'd get certain permissions from movies, however far-fetched. They could break things, scream, & tackle, could bleed, & expose their genitals, could laugh, & cry, could eat shit or could sparkle or swelter or otherwise divorce unflattering their trajectories, & disappear, & wander, & more, & better.

They just weren't supposed to leave their bodies perma-
nently, weren't supposed to cut their genitals, poke holes
in the framework of their pelvises & clavicles with needles,
weren't supposed to stuff things down their underwear,
weren't supposed to shoot themselves with medicine or
eat ass as a kind of throaty absolution, weren't supposed to
invent their own forms of torture or become obsessed with
porn that wasn't POV of them taking dick or only be able to
look if they imagined they were a little boy being dominated
by an adult man because that's all they could imagine was
viable to a little girl/boy because who would ever want *that/
them* in broad daylight but paedophiles or deviants who
stalked women at night time (*not* lunch time). This was the
kind of punk I practiced, the kind about the fissure between
action & language, of Michel Foucault's *parrhesia* – the flim-
sy yet fearless speech of the moral pansy as transposed
through Ovid's *Ars Amatoria* or Oscar Wilde's statements
on "the love that dare not speak its name" in his morality
trial as portrayed by Stephen Fry in the biopic, or Daphne du
Maurier proclaiming in her plagiarism trial (which read like
a training wheels morality trial of sorts loaded with mad-
ly suppressed queer subtext), "… there is nothing worse,
nothing so degrading & shaming than a marriage that has
failed," or how walking down the hallway felt when con-
trolling my buttocks & breath & flinging out my legs to watch
my arms, ambulatory & strange, swing out to match their
crooked rhythm in order to not seem bent, cracked, warped,
or otherwise altered or alterable, to seem as "normal" as

18

possible in whatever ways I could, knowing all the while I was failing & then looking cockeyed from a corner at both of my strange gorgeous teachers, who were others' mothers & never would love some*thing* like me.

Punk made structurally judicious & socially viable for me this plight through the sentient & various institutions that had become of such exceptionally annoying people as Courtney Love, St. Vincent, Hillary Clinton, Virginie Despentes, Kathleen Hanna, Gloria Steinem, Valerie Solanas, Marina Abramović, Miranda July, Mary Wollstonecraft, Sylvia Plath, & Shulamith Firestone – otherwise known as the whitest women on earth. Then the less annoying, presumably drunker or at the very least looser women*, etc., like Billie Holiday, Anne Sexton, Joan Armatrading, Lizzy Mercier Descloux, Kidada Jones, Holly Woodlawn, Anita Lane, The Slits, PJ Harvey, Gia, Dusty Springfield, Edna St. Vincent Millay, Pina Bausch, Anna Calvi, Kim Gordon, Grace Jones, Betty Davis, Beverly Glenn-Copeland, Bette Midler, Team Dresch, Djuna Barnes, Debora Kay Iyall, Carole Pope, Claude Cahun, H.D., &, finally, THE ANGELS; Buffy Sainte-Marie, Poly Styrene, Sister Mary Corita, Alice Coltrane, Alta, Amber Hollibaugh, Dionne Warwick, Leontyne Price, Karen Carpenter, Chaka Khan, Dorothy Ashby, Venus Xtravaganza, Lubaina Himid, Liz Cotten, Debbie Allen, Jackie Shane, Patricia Highsmith, ESG, Gilda Radner, The Shaggs, Pauline Oliveros, Sean DeLear, June Carter Cash, Sue Tompkins, The Raincoats, Tracy + The Plastics, Jenny Mae, Nico,

Assata Shakur, Suzanne Ciani, June Jordan, Gwendolyn Brooks, Mary Margaret O'Hara, Octavia St. Laurent, & Angela Davis, &, &, &. All these women & idols I drowned in when I was supposed to be doing my homework, soaked in meridians from their heroine chic heroin speak. It was all punk to me & blue heart-fire of the kind necessary to lie in a 5-pointed star & drink belly-up upon the lake of it, a fog of their vapors, cigarette exhaust tipping down my throat like molten chocolate mixed with cum & hazed in my eyes like purple genies possessing me with hopelessly romantic magic ejaculate. They offered an opening: "love this & see what happens." Say what you mean or at least trace the experiment of meaning until you un-stalk the woman, a false representative. Find your own mirror of self to stare back at you & look no further & then *do*, unmask the addiction of standing at a crossroads hoping for people to be with. There was a loneliness so indisputable & indescribable in my youth it's impossible to fathom holding it now or how it even got borne. It merited constant obsession & then collapsed to *re*-merit a deprogramming or *re*-writing my way out & through of seeing & *re*-seeing & *re*-seeing, speaking & *re*-saying & *re*-stating & *re*-starting over & over until, like in a war or a protest, I'd made enough public address to make its repression my bitch again & again as it transgressed my egress, as it transgressed my egress, I *pressed* back, fought back, spawned back, beat back, came back, came back to me.

Out on the street where I often lived once my "real" family stopped tolerating me, there was a perfect playground of randomized distraction & adventure. The whole world was a fabulous archive if you had all the time in the world & nothing to lose from talking to people. The thing about autofiction derived from the psychosocial lingual imperative to force yourself to be an active straight shooter or an autodidact of love discourse, the intercourse of feeling is that you only *play* the pied piper because you're mad & raw & thirsty & solitary as hell. You can know everyone in the world by their first name & still be solitary. You can meet every goal or celebrity you've ever ideated over or idolized & still be solitary, as the world is solitary, as you are solitary in death. You may roll with a crew of drag queen punks & you may frequent the psych wards & you may humble yourself in the "Child Protective Services Office" to protect your parents who don't want any trouble from "the local lunatic" & you may keep on a smile in the classroom even if you're called a pickaninny or a nigger for reading Walt Whitman under your desk, & you may find homeless friends who need more than you can spare, & you may go into the woods with them anyway & play hooky over a bonfire & you may fall out on a roof in snow & be covered 'til frostbite & near hypothermia by winter & you may fall into the arms of your bipolar English teacher & she may lose her job to be "in love with you" until you are sick & you may run off to New York because concerned onlookers/bystanders told you to & you may find in New York more bad world to cling to & that

English teacher may move on & divorce her husband & you may look up to find 10 years later she's long been promoted to the superintendent of your old school district & you may look up 10 years later & find she now runs your old middle school where you first felt the warmth of love in a strange non-direction & you may cringe at the things you've done to get here until you buckle down & stop & you may reassert your value in a world full of sickos & you may say "Ok, what's for breakfast?" to your loving girlfriend who is here too & pure of intention & feeling & willing & you may continue on with your day & you may find that you learn as well as you teach & you may find love again & you may find love again & you may find love again & you may find hope & you may find a place to stay & you may stay there & you may hope & you may love & you may & you may & you & you & you, you & you, you & *you* & *you* & *YOU!* **& YOU!**

When I met Amber Hollibaugh she stretched out to me downward from the Great Hall Stage at Cooper Union where I once went to school & where Abraham Lincoln apparently did a big deal thing I can't remember but is plastered everywhere. She reached out not with her hands but with her eyes, a speck jouissance glinting inside her heart for me because she could read the red tattooed sign on my forehead that said *I found out much too late that my 7th grade English teacher had a wife & was gay &, as a result, my 9th grade English teacher got to me* & she understood wordlessly as all invited keynotes do every audience attendee

22

who reaches up in admiration & intrigue to say, "Thank you,"
that I meant it & mean it still forever from then & to this very
day, sincerely ... **Thank you.**

Published by Monitor Books
September 2023

ISBN 978-1-7395424-0-5

This publication is funded by the North West
Consortium Doctoral Training Partnership, part
of the Arts and Humanities Research Council.

Designed by Joe Hales and Sam Eccles
Printed by Swallowtail Print

Monitor Books Ltd.
Deptford, London

monitorbooks.co.uk

Jordan/Martin Hell is a black trans (2s) artist, writer, & researcher. He is
the author of *CONSTANT VIOLINS* (Arcadia Missa, 2022) as well as many
other speculative novellas, hybrid genre, & critical texts in the CV universe.
His writing on art, etc. & interviews have appeared in *032c*, *Real Review*,
*Mousse Magazine*, & others.